Now I Get It!
Understandings and Misunderstandings

TITLES IN THIS SET

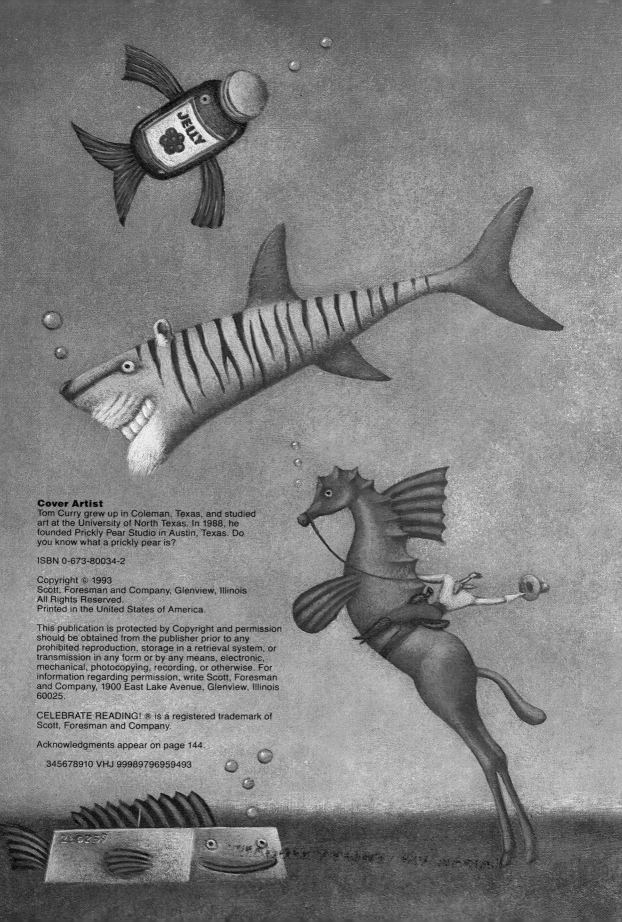

Cover Artist
Tom Curry grew up in Coleman, Texas, and studied art at the University of North Texas. In 1988, he founded Prickly Pear Studio in Austin, Texas. Do you know what a prickly pear is?

ISBN 0-673-80034-2

Acknowledgments appear on page 144.

345678910 VHJ 99989796959493

Now I Get It!

Understandings and Misunderstandings

ScottForesman

A Division of HarperCollins Publishers

Contents

Wondering Why
GENRE STUDY

The Pudding Like a Night on the Sea

by Ann Cameron
illustrations by Ann Strugnell

I'm going to make something special for your mother,"
my father said.

My mother was out shopping. My father was in the kitchen,
looking at the pots and the pans and the jars of this and that.

"What are you going to make?" I said.

"A pudding," he said.

My father is a big man with wild black hair. When he
laughs, the sun laughs in the windowpanes. When he thinks,
you can almost see his thoughts sitting on all the tables
and chairs. When he is angry, me and my little brother, Huey,
shiver to the bottom of our shoes.

"What kind of pudding will you make?" Huey said.

"A wonderful pudding," my father said. "It will taste like a
whole raft of lemons. It will taste like a night on the sea."

7

Then he took down a knife and sliced five lemons in half. He squeezed the first one. Juice squirted in my eye.

"Stand back!" he said, and squeezed again. The seeds flew out on the floor. "Pick up those seeds, Huey!" he said.

Huey took the broom and swept them up.

My father cracked some eggs and put the yolks in a pan and the whites in a bowl. He rolled up his sleeves and pushed back his hair and beat up the yolks. "Sugar, Julian!" he said, and I poured in the sugar.

He went on beating. Then he put in lemon juice and cream and set the pan on the stove. The pudding bubbled and he stirred it fast. Cream splashed on the stove.

"Wipe that up, Huey!" he said.

Huey did.

It was hot by the stove. My father loosened his collar and pushed at his sleeves. The stuff in the pan was getting thicker and thicker. He held the beater up high in the air. "Just right!" he said, and sniffed in the smell of the pudding.

He whipped the egg whites and mixed them into the pudding. The pudding looked softer and lighter than air.

"Done!" he said. He washed all the pots, splashing water on the floor, and wiped the counter so fast his hair made circles around his head.

"Perfect!" he said. "Now I'm going to take a nap. If something important happens, bother me. If nothing important happens, don't bother me. And—the pudding is for your mother. Leave the pudding alone!"

He went to the living room and was asleep in a minute, sitting straight up in his chair.

Huey and I guarded the pudding.

"Oh, it's a wonderful pudding," Huey said.

"With waves on the top like the ocean," I said.

"I wonder how it tastes," Huey said.

"Leave the pudding alone," I said.

"If I just put my finger in—there—I'll know how it tastes," Huey said.

And he did it.

"You did it!" I said. "How does it taste?"

"It tastes like a whole raft of lemons," he said. "It tastes like a night on the sea."

"You've made a hole in the pudding!" I said. "But since you did it, I'll have a taste." And it tasted like a whole night of lemons. It tasted like floating at sea.

"It's such a big pudding," Huey said. "It can't hurt to have a little more."

"Since you took more, I'll have more," I said.

"That was a bigger lick than I took!" Huey said. "I'm going to have more again."

"Whoops!" I said.

"You put in your whole hand!" Huey said. "Look at the pudding you spilled on the floor!"

"I am going to clean it up," I said. And I took the rag from the sink.

"That's not really clean," Huey said.

"It's the best I can do," I said.

"Look at the pudding!" Huey said.

It looked like craters on the moon. "We have to smooth this over," I said. "So it looks the way it did before! Let's get spoons."

And we evened the top of the pudding with spoons, and while we evened it, we ate some more.

"There isn't much left," I said.

"We were supposed to leave the pudding alone," Huey said.

"We'd better get away from here," I said. We ran into our bedroom and crawled under the bed. After a long time we heard my father's voice.

"Come into the kitchen, dear," he said. "I have something for you."

"Why, what is it?" my mother said, out in the kitchen.

Under the bed, Huey and I pressed ourselves to the wall.

"Look," said my father, out in the kitchen. "A wonderful pudding."

"Where is the pudding?" my mother said.

"WHERE ARE YOU BOYS?" my father said. His voice went through every crack and corner of the house.

We felt like two leaves in a storm.

"WHERE ARE YOU? I SAID!" My father's voice
was booming.

Huey whispered to me, "I'm scared."

We heard my father walking slowly through the rooms.

"Huey!" he called. "Julian!"

We could see his feet. He was coming into our room.

He lifted the bedspread. There was his face, and his eyes
like black lightning. He grabbed us by the legs and pulled.
"STAND UP!" he said.

We stood.

"What do you have to tell me?" he said.

"We went outside," Huey said, "and when we came back, the pudding was gone!"

"Then why were you hiding under the bed?" my father said.

We didn't say anything. We looked at the floor.

"I can tell you one thing," he said. "There is going to be some beating here now! There is going to be some whipping!"

The curtains at the window were shaking. Huey was holding my hand.

"Go into the kitchen!" my father said. "Right now!"

We went into the kitchen.

"Come here, Huey!" my father said.

Huey walked toward him, his hands behind his back.

"See these eggs?" my father said. He cracked them and put the yolks in a pan and set the pan on the counter. He stood a chair by the counter. "Stand up here," he said to Huey.

Huey stood on the chair by the counter.

"Now it's time for your beating!" my father said.

Huey started to cry. His tears fell in with the egg yolks.

"Take this!" my father said. My father handed him the egg beater. "Now beat those eggs," he said. "I want this to be a good beating!"

"Oh!" Huey said. He stopped crying. And he beat the egg yolks.

"Now you, Julian, stand here!" my father said.

I stood on a chair by the table.

"I hope you're ready for your whipping!"

I didn't answer. I was afraid to say yes or no.

"Here!" he said, and he set the egg whites in front of me. "I want these whipped and whipped well!"

"Yes, sir!" I said, and started whipping.

My father watched us. My mother came into the kitchen and watched us.

After a while Huey said, "This is hard work."

"That's too bad," my father said. "Your beating's not done!" And he added sugar and cream and lemon juice to Huey's pan and put the pan on the stove. And Huey went on beating.

"My arm hurts from whipping," I said.

"That's too bad," my father said. "Your whipping's not done."

So I whipped and whipped, and Huey beat and beat.

"Hold that beater in the air, Huey!" my father said.

Huey held it in the air.

"See!" my father said. "A good pudding stays on the beater. It's thick enough now. Your beating's done." Then he turned to me. "Let's see those egg whites, Julian!" he said. They were puffed up and fluffy. "Congratulations, Julian!" he said. "Your whipping's done."

He mixed the egg whites into the pudding himself. Then he passed the pudding to my mother.

"A wonderful pudding," she said. "Would you like some, boys?"

"No, thank you," we said.

She picked up a spoon. "Why, this tastes like a whole raft of lemons," she said. "This tastes like a night on the sea."

Thinking About It

1. Julian and Huey didn't mean to eat all of the pudding at first. Think about a time when you got carried away. What happened? How did it turn out?

2. What did the boys' father do when he saw that the pudding had been eaten? Was that the best way to handle it? What else could the father have done about it?

3. The boys misunderstand their father because "whipping" and "beating" can mean more than one thing. What other words do you know which mean more than one thing? How could those words lead to a misunderstanding?

Another Book About Julian

Julian's afraid of bicycles, but he's even more afraid of telling his best friend, Gloria, in *Julian's Glorious Summer* by Ann Cameron.

---

by Beverly Cleary
illustrations by Louis Darling

Ramona's

Great Day

I am *not* a pest," Ramona Quimby told her big sister Beezus.

"Then stop acting like a pest," said Beezus, whose real name was Beatrice. She was standing by the front window waiting for her friend Mary Jane to walk to school with her.

"I am not acting like a pest. I'm singing and skipping," said Ramona, who had only recently learned to skip with both feet. Ramona did not think she was a pest. No matter what others said, she never thought she was a pest. The people who called her a pest were always bigger and so they could be unfair.

Ramona went on with her singing and skipping. "This is a great day, a great day, a great day!" she sang, and to Ramona, who was feeling grown-up in a dress instead of play clothes, this was a great day, the greatest day of her whole life. No longer would she have to sit on her tricycle watching Beezus and Henry Huggins and the rest of the boys and girls in the neighborhood go off to school. Today she was going to school, too. Today she was going to learn to read and write and do all the things that would help her catch up with Beezus.

"Come *on*, Mama!" urged Ramona, pausing in her singing and skipping. "We don't want to be late for school."

"Don't pester, Ramona," said Mrs. Quimby. "I'll get you there in plenty of time."

"I'm *not* pestering," protested Ramona, who never meant to pester. She was not a slowpoke grownup. She was a girl who could not wait. Life was so interesting she had to find out what happened next.

Then Mary Jane arrived. "Mrs. Quimby, would it be all right if Beezus and I take Ramona to kindergarten?" she asked.

"No!" said Ramona instantly. Mary Jane was one of those girls who always wanted to pretend she was a mother and who always wanted Ramona to be the baby. Nobody was going to catch Ramona being a baby on her first day of school.

"Why not?" Mrs. Quimby asked Ramona. "You could walk to school with Beezus and Mary Jane just like a big girl."

"No, I couldn't." Ramona was not fooled for an instant. Mary Jane would talk in that silly voice she used when she was being a mother and take her by the hand and help her across the street, and everyone would think she really was a baby.

"Please, Ramona," coaxed Beezus. "It would be lots of fun to take you in and introduce you to the kindergarten teacher."

"No!" said Ramona, and stamped her foot. Beezus and Mary Jane might have fun, but she wouldn't. Nobody but a genuine grownup was going to take her to school. If she had to, she would

make a great big noisy fuss, and when Ramona made a great big noisy fuss, she usually got her own way. Great big noisy fusses were often necessary when a girl was the youngest member of the family and the youngest person on her block.

"All right, Ramona," said Mrs. Quimby. "Don't make a great big noisy fuss. If that's the way you feel about it, you don't have to walk with the girls. I'll take you."

"Hurry, Mama," said Ramona happily, as she watched Beezus and Mary Jane go out the door. But when Ramona finally got her mother out of the house, she was disappointed to see one of her mother's friends, Mrs. Kemp, approaching with her son Howie and his little sister Willa Jean, who was riding in a stroller. "Hurry, Mama," urged Ramona, not wanting to wait for the Kemps. Because their mothers were friends, she and Howie were expected to get along with one another.

"Hi, there!" Mrs. Kemp called out, so of course Ramona's mother had to wait.

Howie stared at Ramona. He did not like having to get along with her any more than she liked having to get along with him.

Ramona stared back. Howie was a solid-looking boy with curly blond hair. ("Such a waste on a boy," his mother often remarked.) The legs of his new jeans were turned up, and he was wearing a new shirt with long sleeves. He did not look the least bit excited about starting kindergarten. That was the trouble with Howie, Ramona felt. He never got excited. Straight-haired Willa Jean, who was interesting to Ramona because she was so sloppy, blew out a mouthful of wet zwieback crumbs and laughed at her cleverness.

"Today my baby leaves me," remarked Mrs. Quimby with a smile, as the little group proceeded down Klickitat Street toward Glenwood School.

Ramona, who enjoyed being her mother's baby, did not enjoy being called her mother's baby, especially in front of Howie.

"They grow up quickly," observed Mrs. Kemp.

Ramona could not understand why grownups always talked about how quickly children grew up. Ramona thought growing up was the slowest thing there was, slower even than waiting for Christmas to come. She had been waiting years just to get to kindergarten, and the last half hour was the slowest part of all.

When the group reached the intersection nearest Glenwood School, Ramona was pleased to see that Beezus's friend Henry Huggins was the traffic boy in charge of that particular corner. After Henry had led them across the street, Ramona ran off toward the kindergarten, which was a temporary wooden building with its own playground. Mothers and

children were already entering the open door.
Some of the children looked frightened, and one girl
was crying.

"We're late!" cried Ramona. "Hurry!"

Howie was not a boy to be hurried. "I don't see
any tricycles," he said critically. "I don't see any
dirt to dig in."

Ramona was scornful, "This isn't nursery
school. Tricycles and dirt are for nursery school."
Her own tricycle was hidden in the garage, because
it was too babyish for her now that she was going
to school.

Some big first-grade boys ran past yelling,
"Kindergarten babies! Kindergarten babies!"

"We are *not* babies!" Ramona yelled back, as she led her mother into the kindergarten. Once inside she stayed close to her. Everything was so strange, and there was so much to see: the little tables and chairs; the row of cupboards, each with a different picture on the door; the play stove; and the wooden blocks big enough to stand on.

The teacher, who was new to Glenwood School, turned out to be so young and pretty she could not have been a grownup very long. It was rumored she had never taught school before. "Hello, Ramona. My name is Miss Binney," she said, speaking each syllable distinctly as she pinned Ramona's name to her dress. "I am so glad you have come to kindergarten." Then she took Ramona by the hand and led her to one of the little tables and chairs. "Sit here for the present," she said with a smile.

A present! thought Ramona, and knew at once she was going to like Miss Binney.

"Good-by, Ramona," said Mrs. Quimby. "Be a good girl."

As she watched her mother walk out the door, Ramona decided school was going to be even better than she had hoped. Nobody had told her she was going to get a present the very first day. What kind of present could it be, she wondered, trying to remember if Beezus had ever been given a present by her teacher.

Ramona listened carefully while Miss Binney showed Howie to a table, but all her teacher said was, "Howie, I would like you to sit here." Well! thought Ramona. Not everyone is going to get a present so Miss Binney must like me best. Ramona watched and listened as the other boys and girls arrived, but Miss Binney did not tell anyone else he was going to get a present if he sat in a certain chair. Ramona wondered if her present would be wrapped in fancy paper and tied with a ribbon like a birthday present. She hoped so.

As Ramona sat waiting for her present she watched the other children being introduced to Miss Binney by their mothers. She found two members of the morning kindergarten especially interesting. One was a boy named Davy, who was small, thin, and eager. He was the only boy in the class in short pants, and Ramona liked him at once. She liked him so much she decided she would like to kiss him.

The other interesting person was a big girl named Susan. Susan's hair looked like the hair on the girls in the pictures of the old-fashioned stories Beezus liked to read. It was reddish-brown and hung in curls like springs that touched her shoulders and bounced as she walked. Ramona had never seen such curls before. All the curly-haired girls she knew wore their hair short. Ramona put her hand to her own short straight hair, which was an

ordinary brown, and longed to touch that bright, springy hair. She longed to stretch one of those curls and watch it spring back. *Boing!* thought Ramona, making a mental noise like a spring on a television cartoon and wishing for thick, springy, *boing-boing* hair like Susan's.

Howie interrupted Ramona's admiration of Susan's hair. "How soon do you think we get to go out and play?" he asked.

"Maybe after Miss Binney gives me the present," Ramona answered. "She said she was going to give me one."

"How come she's going to give you a present?" Howie wanted to know. "She didn't say anything about giving me a present."

"Maybe she likes me best," said Ramona.

This news did not make Howie happy. He turned to the next boy and said, *"She's* going to get a present."

Ramona wondered how long she would have to sit there to get the present. If only Miss Binney understood how hard waiting was for her! When the last child had been welcomed and the last tearful mother had departed, Miss Binney gave a little talk about the rules of the kindergarten and showed the class the door that led to the bathroom. Next she assigned each person a little cupboard. Ramona's cupboard had a picture of a yellow duck on the door, and Howie's had a green frog. Miss Binney explained that their hooks in the cloakroom were marked with the same pictures. Then she asked the class to follow her quietly into the cloakroom to find their hooks.

Difficult though waiting was for her, Ramona did not budge. Miss Binney had not told her to get up and go into the cloakroom for her present. She had told her to sit for the present, and Ramona was going to sit until she got it. She would sit as if she were glued to the chair.

Howie scowled at Ramona as he returned from the cloakroom and said to another boy, "The teacher is going to give *her* a present."

Naturally the boy wanted to know why. "I don't know," admitted Ramona. "She told me that if I sat here I would get a present. I guess she likes me best."

By the time Miss Binney returned from the cloakroom, word had spread around the classroom that Ramona was going to get a present.

Next Miss Binney taught the class the words of a puzzling song about "the dawnzer lee light," which Ramona did not understand because she did not know what a dawnzer was. "Oh, say can you see by the dawnzer lee light," sang Miss Binney, and Ramona decided that a dawnzer was another word for a lamp.

When Miss Binney had gone over the song several times, she asked the class to stand and sing it with her. Ramona did not budge. Neither did Howie and some of the others, and Ramona knew they were hoping for a present, too. Copycats, she thought.

"Stand up straight like good Americans," said Miss Binney so firmly that Howie and the others reluctantly stood up.

Ramona decided she would have to be a good American sitting down.

"Ramona," said Miss Binney, "aren't you going to stand with the rest of us?"

Ramona thought quickly. Maybe the question was some kind of test, like a test in a fairy tale. Maybe Miss Binney was testing her to see if she could get her out of her seat. If she failed the test, she would not get the present.

"I can't," said Ramona.

Miss Binney looked puzzled, but she did not insist that Ramona stand while she led the class through the dawnzer song. Ramona sang along with the others and hoped that her present came next, but when the song ended, Miss Binney made no mention of the present. Instead she picked up a book. Ramona decided that at last the time had come to learn to read.

Miss Binney stood in front of her class and began to read aloud from *Mike Mulligan and His Steam Shovel,* a book that was a favorite of Ramona's because, unlike so many books for her age, it was neither quiet and sleepy nor sweet and pretty. Ramona, pretending she was glued to her chair, enjoyed hearing the story again and listened quietly with the rest of the kindergarten to the story of Mike Mulligan's old-fashioned steam shovel, which proved its worth by digging the basement for the new town hall of Poppersville in a single day beginning at dawn and ending as the sun went down.

As Ramona listened a question came into her mind, a question that had often puzzled her about the books that were read to her. Somehow books always left out one of the most important things anyone would want to know. Now that Ramona was in school, and school was a place for learning, perhaps Miss Binney could answer the question. Ramona waited quietly until her teacher had finished the story, and then she raised her hand the way Miss Binney had told the class they should raise their hands when they wanted to speak in school.

Joey, who did not remember to raise his hand, spoke out. "That's a good book."

Miss Binney smiled at Ramona, and said, "I like the way Ramona remembers to raise her hand when she has something to say. Yes, Ramona?"

Ramona's hopes soared. Her teacher had smiled at her. "Miss Binney, I want to know—how did Mike Mulligan go to the bathroom when he was digging the basement of the town hall?"

Miss Binney's smile seemed to last longer than smiles usually last. Ramona glanced uneasily around and saw that others were waiting with interest for the answer. Everybody wanted to know how Mike Mulligan went to the bathroom.

"Well—" said Miss Binney at last. "I don't really know, Ramona. The book doesn't tell us."

"I always wanted to know, too," said Howie, without raising his hand, and others murmured in agreement. The whole class, it seemed, had been wondering how Mike Mulligan went to the bathroom.

"Maybe he stopped the steam shovel and climbed out of the hole he was digging and went to a service station," suggested a boy named Eric.

"He couldn't. The book says he had to work as fast as he could all day." Howie pointed out. "It doesn't say he stopped."

Miss Binney faced the twenty-nine earnest members of the kindergarten, all of whom wanted to know how Mike Mulligan went to the bathroom.

"Boys and girls," she began, and spoke in her clear, distinct way. "The reason the book does not tell us how Mike Mulligan went to the bathroom is that it is not an important part of the story. The story is about digging the basement of the town hall, and that is what the book tells us."

Miss Binney spoke as if this explanation ended the matter, but the kindergarten was not convinced. Ramona knew and the rest of the class knew that knowing how to go to the bathroom *was* important. They were surprised that Miss Binney did not understand, because she had showed them the bathroom the very first thing. Ramona could see there were some things she was not going to learn in school, and along with the rest of the class she stared reproachfully at Miss Binney.

The teacher looked embarrassed, as if she knew she had disappointed her kindergarten. She recovered quickly, closed the book, and told the class that if they would walk quietly out to the playground she would teach them a game called Gray Duck.

Ramona did not budge. She watched the rest of the class leave the room and admired Susan's *boing-boing* curls as they bounced about her shoulders, but she did not stir from her seat. Only Miss Binney could unstick the imaginary glue that held her there.

"Don't you want to learn to play Gray Duck, Ramona?" Miss Binney asked.

Ramona nodded. "Yes, but I can't."

"Why not?" asked Miss Binney.

"I can't leave my seat," said Ramona. When Miss Binney looked blank, she added, "Because of the present."

"What present?" Miss Binney seemed so genuinely puzzled that Ramona became uneasy. The teacher sat down in the little chair next to Ramona's, and said, "Tell me why you can't play Gray Duck."

Ramona squirmed, worn out with waiting. She had an uneasy feeling that something had gone wrong someplace. "I want to play Gray Duck, but you—" she stopped, feeling that she might be about to say the wrong thing.

"But I what?" asked Miss Binney.

"Well . . . uh . . . you said if I sat here I would get a present," said Ramona at last, "but you didn't say how long I had to sit here."

If Miss Binney had looked puzzled before, she now looked baffled. "Ramona, I don't understand—" she began.

"Yes, you did," said Ramona, nodding. "You told me to sit here for the present, and I have been sitting here ever since school started and you haven't given me a present."

Miss Binney's face turned red and she looked so embarrassed that Ramona felt completely confused. Teachers were not supposed to look that way.

Miss Binney spoke gently. "Ramona, I'm afraid we've had a misunderstanding."

Ramona was blunt. "You mean I don't get a present?"

"I'm afraid not," admitted Miss Binney. "You see 'for the present' means for now. I meant that I wanted you to sit here for now, because later I may have the children sit at different desks."

"Oh." Ramona was so disappointed she had nothing to say. Words were so puzzling. *Present* should mean a present just as *attack* should mean to stick tacks in people.

By now all the children were crowding around the door to see what had happened to their teacher. "I'm so sorry," said Miss Binney. "It's all my fault. I should have used different words."

"That's all right," said Ramona, ashamed to have the class see that she was not going to get a present after all.

Thinking About It

1. Ramona has some misunderstandings on her first day of school. When have you ever thought someone was saying one thing when they really meant something else? What happened?

2. Why does Beezus call Ramona a pest? Do you think she's a pest? Walk to school with Beezus one morning and discuss this with her.

3. It's Ramona's second day in kindergarten. Can you make it a better day for Ramona? Tell what might happen to Ramona on her second day in kindergarten.

Ramona's Growing Up!

She's not in kindergarten anymore, but Ramona still gets into some funny messes in *Ramona Quimby, Age 8* by Beverly Cleary.

Sing Me a Song of Teapots and Trumpets

by N. M. Bodecker

Sing me a song
of teapots and trumpets:
Trumpots and teapets
And tippets and taps,
trippers and trappers
and jelly bean wrappers
and pigs in pajamas
with zippers and snaps.

Sing me a song
of sneakers and snoopers:
Snookers and sneapers
and snappers and snacks,
snorkels and snarkles,
a seagull that gargles,
and gargoyles and gryphons
and other knickknacks.

Sing me a song
of parsnips and pickles:
Picsnips and parkles
and pumpkins and pears,
plumbers and mummers
and kettle drum drummers
and plum jam (yum-yum jam)
all over their chairs.

Sing me a song—
but never you mind it!
I've had enough
of this nonsense. Don't cry.
Criers and fliers
and onion ring fryers—
It's more than I want to put up with!
Good-by!

Mom Can't See Me

by Sally Hobart Alexander

photographs by George Ancona

Nine years ago, when I was born, Mom could pick me out
of a bunch of babies. I had the biggest feet. Mom had
to find me that way because she can't see.

When she was twenty-six, blood vessels inside her
eyes started breaking. The blood didn't show, but soon it
made her blind.

Some blind people can see colors or blurry blotches,
but my mom can't see any of those things. She's totally
blind and can't even tell if a light is on or off. She doesn't
see black, just smoky white or gray. Once I put a scarf
over my eyes and tried out being blind. I got lots of
bumps, just like Mom, so I took off the blindfold. Mom
can't take off her blindness. She doesn't seem sad about
it, just frustrated when she can't find things quickly.

Except for her eyes, Mom looks completely normal. She wears sunglasses, even in the house. They make her prettier and safer from open cupboard doors and other things that could hit her.

When Dad first saw Mom in those glasses, he thought she looked like a movie star. Later he learned that she was funny and independent, too, and asked her to marry him. My big brother, Joel, makes a face when he hears this story, but I love it and tell everybody.

When I was four months old, Mom says I already understood that she was blind. At a "Mothers' Day Out" program, other babies smiled when their mothers came for them. When Mom came for me, I squeaked and gurgled and made all kinds of noises so she could find me. I still make noise for Mom, especially when Joel silently teases me. If I screech, Mom comes to the rescue.

Not everybody understands about having a blind mom. I wish they did. My friends always nod or point when they talk. Since Mom can't see what they're doing, I have to explain. I feel like a translator.

Mom does some things differently, but mostly she's like other mothers. She walks with Marit, her guide dog. Marit leads Mom around telephone poles and anything else that might bump her.

I'm glad that Marit can go everywhere with us—on buses, to restaurants, to school, even in a canoe.

Joel and I play with Marit when she stops working. As soon as her harness is off, Marit drops her toy frog at our feet and barks till we play.

When I was little, Mom made *me* wear a kind of harness and leash, too, so she could feel where I was. After the first morning of nursery school, my new friend, Charlotte, asked her mother, "Why is the lady pulling Leslie on a rope?"

Mom used to put jingly bells on my shoes so she could hear me. When I wanted to stay longer at nursery school with Charlotte, I took off my shoes. Then Mom couldn't find me.

I still do things that Mom doesn't know about right away. If Dad's not home, I switch the light back on to read way after bedtime. Once I sneaked some cookies so quietly that Mom couldn't possibly have heard the lid clang. But then she asked, "Why are you eating chocolate chip cookies so close to dinner?" I forgot that she could smell them on my breath.

When we were younger, Mom read to Joel and me, but she had to use books with braille bumps, as well as print and pictures. Our favorite was *The Little Engine That Could.*

Braille is hard to learn. I tried it. Even when I remembered how many dots stood for a letter, I couldn't always feel each one. Mom's fingers weren't that speedy at reading it, so sometimes we said the printed words before Mom could read the braille ones: "I think I can. I think I can."

Mom uses braille recipes and braille labels
when she cooks. For baking, we use a braille timer so
that our cookies don't burn. "May I lick the bowl?"
I always ask. "Of course, Leslie," Mom says.
She doesn't know how much of the batter I've
already eaten.

Most mothers drive, but not ours. She walks us places or takes us by bus. On long trips, to our piano lessons and back, for instance, she tells us parts of an exciting story like *Treasure Island.*

Mom can borrow huge books on cassette tapes from a library. Whenever Dad takes us out in the car, we play them. And on camping trips we all like to listen in our tent, even Marit.

Mom takes me to the movies, I tell her what's going on in the silent parts. If they're exciting, she has to remind me to whisper.

She takes me to musicals. *My Fair Lady* is the one we like best, and we know the words to all the songs. We sing them, very loudly, while Mom curls my hair.

Mom and I take tap-dancing lessons together. At my cousin's wedding we tapped to the tune of "Tea for Two."

I also dance when Mom plays the piano. There's braille sheet music, but Mom plays by ear. Sometimes Mom and I play duets, the way she and her dad did years ago. I always open the front door so the people on my street can listen.

At my gymnastics class, Mom can't tell my thumps from anybody else's. I'm still glad she's there. Once a girl in my class asked Mom, "Can you see anything?" Her mother scolded her, but I said it was okay. Joel and I ask other handicapped people questions. We think it's being interested, not rude.

On Saturdays Joel and I ride our bikes. Mom and Dad come along on their two-seater. "Mom pedals, and I steer," Dad always says. The bike is so unusual that everybody stares at us, but they don't know that Mom is blind.

Mom plays baseball with Joel and me. Joel calls her the "designated hitter." She can't catch, but if she throws the ball up herself, she sure can hit.

She takes me swimming. We like the neighborhood pool best because the lanes are roped off and she can't crash into any other swimmers.

On Tuesdays Mom volunteers at my school. It makes me feel important. She talks about books in the reading classes. Sometimes kids tell her stories, which she types into books for them.

Before she became blind, Mom taught elementary school. Now she's a writer. She has a computer that speaks every word she types. When I interrupt her at the computer, she makes it say, "Give me a smooch, Leslie."

Until Mom got the computer, she used a regular typewriter. I read her chapters onto tape. Once Mom typed a story all over my math homework. Luckily my teacher could find my answers, and she read Mom's story to the class.

I guess Mom makes more mistakes than other mothers. But mostly they're silly ones, like spraying lemon furniture polish, instead of starch, when she was ironing my dress.

Mom made the funniest mistake at the airport. She threw her arms around a man who sounded like her brother. It was the pilot, but he laughed and hugged Mom back.

Sometimes her mistakes embarrass me, like when she keeps talking to a clerk who's walked away. I nudge her and say, "She's gone."

Or when Mom answers people who are not even talking to her. Once, in a hotel, a man said, "Oh, you're beautiful!" Mom thanked him, but he explained, "I was talking to your dog."

At Joel's soccer games, all she hears are twelve-year-olds puffing and thudding down the field. When the crowd cheers and I say, "Joel scored," she jumps up and screams, even if the rest of the people have gotten quiet again. This makes me cringe. But the worst was the time I goofed and told her Joel had scored when he hadn't. Mom jumped up and yelled, "Way to go, Joel!" Joel's face got all red, and he called right from the field, "Eben scored, Mom, not me!"

When I tell Mom I'm embarrassed, she pulls my nose and says, "That's what parents are for, embarrassing their kids!"

I think I'm a little different from kids with regular mothers. I don't always laugh at jokes that call somebody blind just for not seeing something. To me that's not exactly funny.

I have to remember things better. If I forget to pack my lunch or homework, Mom has to ride two buses to get to my school.

I help Mom more, reading to her and telling her if her lipstick is crooked. I also wash fingerprints from the walls and stains from my clothes. Mom pays me for being her special helper.

Charlotte thinks it's funny that Joel and I put Mom's hand on things we describe to her, like a design I created or a puppet Joel made.

I hold Mom's hand, sit on her lap, and hug her a lot. I tell Charlotte it's the same as her smiling at her mom, but I think it's better. Joel says he's too old for this mushy stuff, but Mom hugs him, anyway. "Blind parents get special privileges," she says. Mom plans to hug us till we're forty-five.

"When I'm forty-five," I tell Joel, "I bet there'll be a way to fix Mom's eyes." He doubts it. But he wishes Mom could see him when he's swimming freestyle or zooming on his skateboard. I sure wish Mom could see, especially when there's something too wonderful to describe, like the Grand Canyon or Niagara Falls.

I wish she could see me, too. Mom says she'd love to get a little peek at me or Joel or Dad. Since she can't, she says she takes a double share of

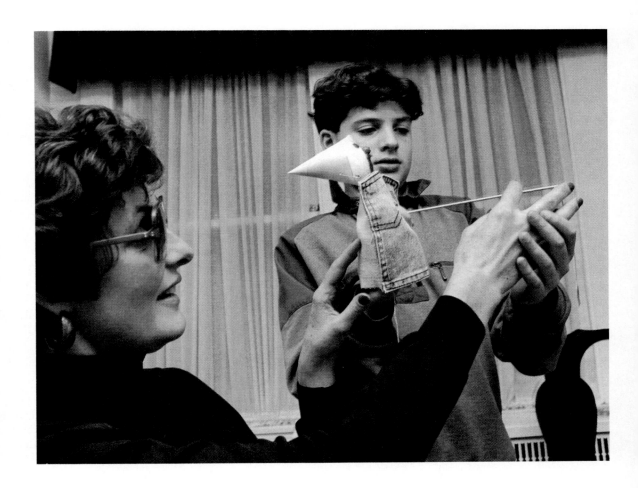

touching and hearing us. My aunt tells her I look just
the way Mom did when she was a "nine-year-old
squirt with a gap between her new teeth." So I guess
Mom has a pretty good picture of me. Anyway, every
time I have a birthday, I make two wishes over the
candles—one for me and one for Mom.

I tell Joel I'm scared about becoming blind some
day. He says you can't catch blindness like chicken
pox. Besides, our doctor says we can't inherit Mom's
kind of blindness.

Mom sure doesn't seem scared. Once she did
something that none of my friends' mothers ever
did. She climbed all across a rope course, high in
the trees. I was really nervous watching her, but
Marit was even worse. She barked the whole time.
Afterward I was very proud. Mom was so brave.

Mom sure is silly, the way she wakes me up
for school in the morning and pretends to gobble
me up or kiss me and tickle me all over.

She says she can *still* pick me out of a bunch
of kids. I'm the skinniest girl on the block, and
I still have the biggest feet.

A Message from Mom

by Sally Hobart Alexander

S. Alexander

One of the best things about writing books is that I am asked to speak at schools. The children bombard me with questions, mostly about blindness.

The most common question I get is how do I keep from getting hurt or lost when I walk outside. Three things make it possible:

1. my sense of touch,
2. my sense of hearing,
3. my guide dog.

Before I got my dog, I used a cane outside. Canes help me to feel hedges, walkways, curbs, and parking meters. My feet feel the surface of the pavement, and I locate places by the roughness or smoothness in front of me.

More important than my sense of touch is my sense of hearing. Although traffic is a danger, it is also a friend. It tells me when to cross a street. If the cars are moving with me, I know the light is green. If they are flowing in front, the light is red.

Sounds, like my voice or footsteps, bounce off hard surfaces, making an echo. You can see how this works. Close your eyes while a friend places a book above, beside, or in front of your head. Make a sound. You should be able to locate the book. In the same way, I can locate a building, movie marquee, or telephone pole.

Another help to me is my guide dog, Marit. She is trained to follow my orders, "right, left, forward." She cannot read signs or tell the color of a traffic light. I memorize the street patterns and keep track of where we are. But without a word from me, Marit leads me around low branches, sidewalk construction, or anything that would hurt me.

Of course, it doesn't work to whisper to her, "Marit, ice cream shop, please."

Thinking About It

1. As you read and looked at the pictures in *Mom Can't See Me*, what did you think about? Which picture is most interesting? If you stepped into it, what would you say and do?
2. Sally Hobart Alexander has many ways of getting along without her sight. What are some of the things she does to make use of her other senses? What works best?
3. What could you invent to help Sally Hobart Alexander?

Animal Talk

by Dorothy Hinshaw Patent

NORTHERN ORIOLE
Icterus galbula

MOUNTAIN BLUEBIRD
Siala currucoides

HAPPINESS

SURPRISE

ANGER

SADNESS

WONDER

People talk to each other every day. When you tell a friend to meet you at the playground after school, your friend understands and joins you there. Animals, too, need ways to tell each other things, or *communicate* (Kuh-MEW-nih-kate).

There are different ways of communicating. People don't just use their voices. They also show how they feel with a smile, a frown, a friendly pat on the back, or a kiss. Like people, animals need to "talk" to one another. But animals don't have words. So how do they communicate?

WILD HORSE
Equus Caballus

COLLIE
Canus familiaris

BROWN
RECLUSE
SPIDER
Loxosceles reclusa

JAVANESE
felis domesticus

SPECIAL WAYS OF COMMUNICATING

Dogs bark or growl. Horses neigh. Male crickets rub their wings together to make the chirping sounds that attract females. Some fish grate their teeth together to make sounds.

Many animals use their tails to show how they feel. Some crabs and spiders wave their legs in special patterns to attract a mate.

Dogs, horses, and cats use their ears not only to hear but also to show how they are feeling. They flatten them back if they are angry or let them stand straight up if they are alert, eager, or happy.

BLACK-CAPPED CHICKADEE *Parus atricapillus*

CARDINAL *Cardinalis Cardinalis*

WHITE-CROWNED SPARROW *Zonotrichia leucophrys*

SINGING BIRDS

Have you ever heard the lovely song of a sparrow in the morning? When birds sing, they are not just making beautiful music. They are communicating.

While female birds can chirp, it is usually the males that truly "sing." Sometimes they sing to attract a mate—"This is my place. Here I am, ready to start a family."

Once a songbird and his mate get together, the male sings for a different reason. Now he is letting other birds of his kind know where his home is. His song says, "This is my place. Stay away."

WOOD THRUSH
Hylocichla mustelina

COMMON
REDPOLL
Carduelis flammea

MOCKINGBIRD
Mimus polyglottos

AMERICAN ROBIN
Turdus migratorius

Each kind of songbird has its own special song. When you hear certain notes, you know that you are listening to a white-crowned sparrow. A meadowlark has a very different tune. Each bird can recognize when another bird of its own kind is singing.

When birds sing, they are not using real language the way humans do. While humans can speak hundreds of different languages, each kind of bird has only one "language" with a few "words."

WHITE-CROWNED
SPARROW
*Zonotrichia
Leucophrys*

EASTERN
MEADOWLARK
Sturnella magna

YELLOW-HEADED
BLACKBIRD
Xanthocephalus Xanthocephalus

RED-WINGED
BLACKBIRD
Agelaius pheoniceus

We can tell each other all kinds of things with words. But birds have only a few messages they can get across. A person can say the same thing in different ways. "Please come to my birthday party on Saturday" means the same as "Saturday is my birthday. Can you come to my party?" But a bird has only one way of saying "This is my place."

FLASHING FIREFLIES

Many animals depend more on sight than sound to get messages across. The sparkling flashes of fireflies across a nighttime meadow are beautiful to us. But they provide important information to the fireflies.

During the mating season, female fireflies often perch on the tops of plants, while the males fly above them, flashing bright signals.

COMMON FIREFLY
Photinus pyratis

There are many kinds of fireflies, and each kind has its own special flashing code. When a female sees the proper code, she waits just the right amount of time. Then she flashes back.

When a male sees a flash from the grass at the right time, he turns and heads to the spot. Here is a female of his kind, ready to mate with him. As he approaches, he flashes again and she answers. When he gets close, he lands on the grass and walks toward her, flashing as he comes. Then they mate.

TRAILING ANTS

Have you ever watched a trail of ants marching across the kitchen floor toward a bit of food, or heading out from a woodland nest? The ants are traveling in both directions, hurrying along their way. Some of them are going out from the nest. Others are returning with something to eat.

How do the ants know where to go to find the food?

Many ants live in big nests underground, or above the ground in wood. There are thousands of them in each of these big family homes. Some of the ants wander away from the nest looking for food. They are called scouts.

When a scout finds a juicy piece of fruit, a dead grasshopper, or some other food, it heads for home. As it returns, the scout leaves a trail with a special chemical released from the rear end of its body.

Back at the nest, other ants smell the fresh trail left by the scout. They follow it back to the food.

After collecting as much as they can carry, they scurry back to the nest, leaving more of the chemical trail as they go.

Every ant that returns with food leaves a trail, just like the scout. More and more ants head out and return with good things to eat.

Once all the food is gone, returning ants no longer leave any scent on their way home. The trail smell gets weaker and weaker, and soon the ants don't waste any more time following it.

WHITE ARCTIC WOLF
Canis lupus arctos

A LOVING TOUCH

Wolves live in very close groups called packs. They have many different ways of communicating with each other.

They do so by howling, moving their ears and tails, and using smell. But for wolves, touch is also a very important way of expressing feelings.

GRAY OR TIMBER WOLF
Canis lupus

In each wolf pack, one male and one female are the leaders. The other wolves are usually their offspring from different years.

When one of the leaders has been away for a while and returns, the other wolves dash over to greet the returning wolf.

They nuzzle the leader. They lick at his or her face and push their bodies as close together as they can. Their greetings seem much like humans' hugs and kisses.

SEA LION
Zalophus
Californianus

WAYS OF "TALKING"

You can see that animals communicate in many ways. They use sight, sound, smell, and touch. Next time you go for a walk in the park or to the zoo, see if you can figure out how the animals you see are "talking" to each other.

Thinking About It

WESTERN TANAGER
Piranga ludoviciana

1. Animals communicate with each other in many ways. How do you communicate with animals, and how do they communicate with you?

2. What are some of the reasons that animals communicate? Do you ever communicate for the same reasons? What do you say or do to communicate those ideas to other people?

3. If real animals could talk to people, what would they say to us?

Other Ways to Understand Animals

A baby dolphin learns about the excitement of life in the sea in *Dolphin* by Robert A. Morris.

ON THE TRAIL

BY KATHLEEN V. KUDLINSKI

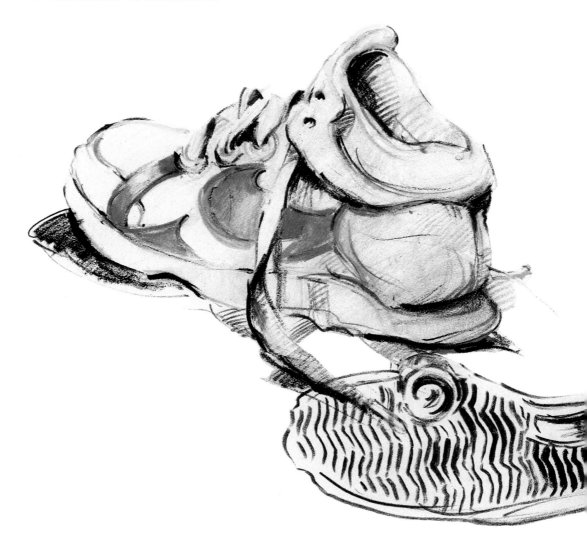

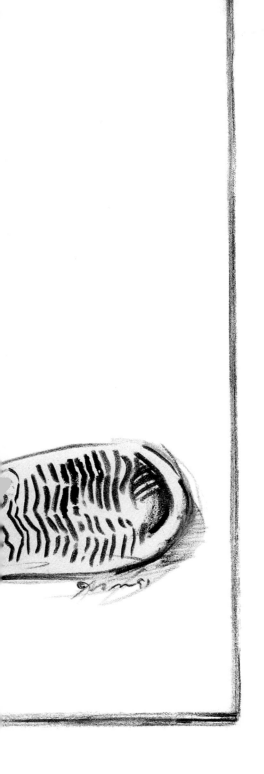

CLUES

"Will you *please* clean up this mess?"

How many times have you heard that? Did you ever wonder how your folks always know whom to blame?

You are probably pretty sloppy about leaving clues behind. Who else would leave handprints like yours on the refrigerator, your favorite cereal on the counter, your dirty clothes on the floor, a world-class mess in your own room?

Your folks know whom to blame because they find the clues you leave behind and they know how to read them.

Animals are pretty sloppy about leaving clues behind, too. If you know where to look, you can find their handprints, dirty dishes, old clothing, and messy rooms.

It's easy to watch how cats, dogs, or other pets behave, but wild animals are shy. They hide so well that most people never even know they are around. You can find out about them from the clues they leave behind. And you can get to see them, too.

T R A C K S

Your dirty handprints or muddy
footprints can give you away.
Animals leave hand- and footprint
clues, too. They leave prints if
their paws are dirty. They leave
tracks if they step on something
soft. Each kind of animal makes
a different kind of track.

Can you guess from these
clues who was here?

To read tracks, you need to
know how animals' feet are shaped,
and how they walk and move.

Furry animals make three
different kinds of tracks because
of how they walk. Horses and
deer walk on the very tips of their
toes, like ballerinas. Instead of
toenails, these animals have
hooves. Their tracks are hoof
marks. Horses' hooves leave one
mark, shaped like the letter **U**.
Deer and cows have two hooves
on each foot.

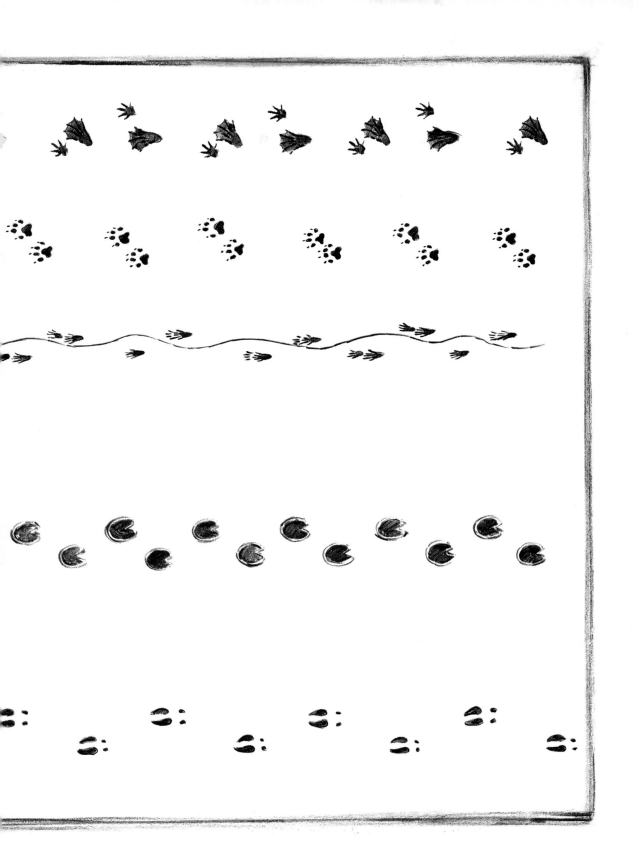

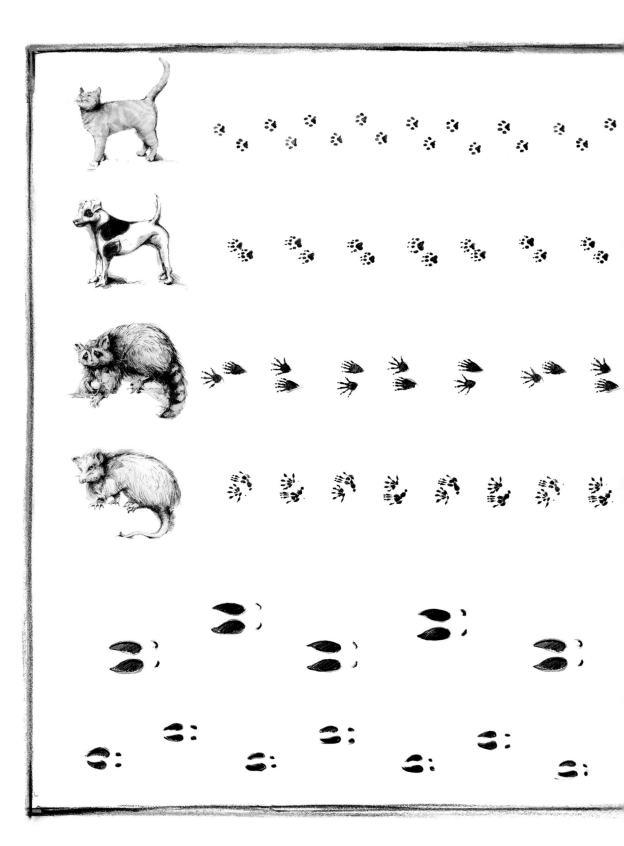

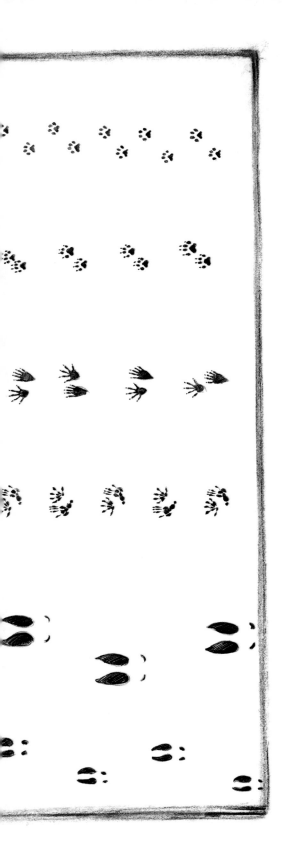

Cats' and dogs' legs are made so that they walk on their "tippy toes." There is never a heel mark in their tracks. Dog and cat prints seem almost alike, but if you look closely, you can tell them apart. In a dog's track there are tiny marks in front of each toe. These are made by the dog's claws. Cats hold their claws up when they walk. That way, their claws stay sharp and make no mark in a track.

Opossums and raccoons walk on flat feet, like we do. Their front paws leave tracks that look like tiny handprints. Their back paws look like our feet, but with extra-long toes. Both animals are about the same size. How can you tell their tracks apart? Opossums walk with their thumbs and chubby fingers spread wide. Raccoons walk with their skinny fingers and thumbs held closer together. Can you tell these apart?

Some furry animals leave tracks of almost the same shape, but they are different sizes. Bigger animals have bigger feet. Which animal made which track?

Bird tracks all look alike at first, too. You can tell about where a bird lives by looking at its tracks. Birds that live in the water leave tracks with web marks between the toes. Ducks and geese leave this kind of track.

Birds that spend a lot of time on the ground walk the way we do, moving one foot at a time. Pigeons and starlings are walkers, and make tracks one after another.

Other birds spend most of their time hopping from branch to branch in treetops. They don't know how to walk. When they land on the ground, they hop, making tracks in neat pairs. Sparrows and finches are hopping birds.

SHEDDINGS

If the dirty clothes on the floor are yours, it's easy to guess that you were the one who dropped them there.

Animals leave things behind, too. These are the easiest wildlife clues to read. Only a snake can shed a snakeskin. All feathers come from birds. Can you guess who left behind these "dirty clothes"?

Many animals shed their fur. Sometimes you can find wild animal hairs in old birds' nests or lining rabbits' nests in the grass. It is hard to see a hair outdoors. Indoors it is easy to find pet dog or cat fur gathered under sofas or on soft chairs.

Feathers are much easier to find than hairs. Every bird has hundreds of feathers that it sheds at least once a year. In North America, shedding time is late summer, after baby birds have grown. Only a few feathers drop out at a time and new ones grow back quickly. That way birds always have enough feathers to fly away from danger.

If you find a feather, its color and pattern can tell you what kind of bird it came from. The feather's shape can tell you where it grew on the bird. Tiny, fuzzy "down" feathers are a bird's warm undershirt. These feathers don't seem to have any stem, or "shaft," up the middle.

Body feathers cover the down. These feathers are small, but do have shafts. Wing and tail feathers are longer and stiffer. If the shaft goes right down the middle of the feather, it came from a bird's tail. If it is closer to one edge, it came from a wing.

Skins that snakes have shed make good collections. Snakes shed whenever they have grown too big for their skins. You can find skins any time of year that snakes are awake. A snake starts shedding its skin by rubbing its lips against rough ground or rocks. The skin peels off inside out, like a sock pulled off your foot. New, fresh skin and scales are ready underneath, so the snake just leaves its old skin behind.

Insects and spiders shed their skins, too. Like snakes, their old skins get too tight as they grow. When a new skin is ready underneath, the old skin splits down the back. The insect or spider pulls itself out through the hole. The shed skins keep the shape of the animal, with every leg and hair in place. Mice like to eat these sheddings, so you don't often see this animal clue.

You can probably find all kinds of animal clues where you live. Even in the city there are animals that leave tracks and traces you can see if you look carefully. Did you ever imagine there were so many ways to discover animals? Each track, feather, and skin gives you important information about the kind of animal that left it behind. You can be an animal detective. Try keeping track of the animals in your neighborhood. You might be surprised at what you find!

THINKING ABOUT IT

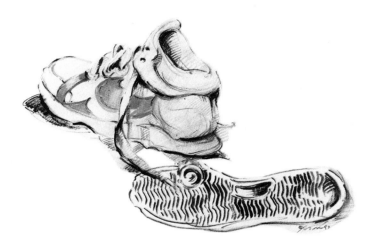

1. This article told about many different animal signs. Which of these signs have you seen where you live? Which animals do you think left the signs behind?

2. Your school library gets a ton of new books. The librarian asks you to help her find all of the nonfiction books. How can you tell when you've found one? What will you look for?

3. You are going to write a new nonfiction book. What will you write about? What title will you give your book?

THE NIGHT
OF THE STARS

by Douglas Gutiérrez
illustrations by María Fernanda Oliver

Translated by Carmen Diana Dearden

Long, long ago, in a town
   that was neither near nor far,
      there lived a man
         who did not like the night.

During the day, in the sunlight, he worked
weaving baskets, watching over his
animals and watering his vegetables.
Often he would sing.
But as soon as the sun set behind the mountain,
this man who did not like the night
would become sad, for his world suddenly
turned gray, dark and black.
"Night again! Horrible night!" he would cry out.
He would then pick up his baskets, light his
lamp and shut himself up in his house.
Sometimes he would look out the window, but
there was nothing to see in the dark sky.
So he would put out his lamp
and go to bed.

One day, at sunset,

    the man went to the mountain.

    Night was beginning to cover the blue sky.

    The man climbed to the

highest peak and shouted:

           "Please, night. Stop!"

And the night did stop for a moment.

    "What is it?" she asked in a soft, deep voice.

    "Night, I don't like you. When you come, the light goes
away and the colors disappear. Only the darkness remains."

    "You're right," answered the night. "It is so."

    "Tell me, where do you take the light?" asked the man.

    "It hides behind me, and I cannot do anything
about it," replied the night. "I'm very sorry."

    The night finished stretching and
covered the world with darkness.

The man came down from the mountain and went to bed.

But he could not sleep.

Nor during the next day could he work.

All he could think about was his conversation with the night.

And in the afternoon, when the light began to disappear again, he said to himself:

"I know what to do."

Once more
he went to the mountain.
The night was like an immense
awning, covering all things.
When at last he reached the
highest point on the mountain,
the man stood on his tiptoes,
and with his finger poked a hole
in the black sky.
A pinprick of light flickered through the hole.
The man who did not like the night was delighted.
He poked holes all over the sky.
Here, there, everywhere, and all over the sky
little points of light appeared.

Amazed now at what he could do,
the man made a fist
and punched it through the darkness.
A large hole opened up,
and a huge, round light,
almost like a grapefruit, shone through.
All the escaping light cast a brilliant glow
at the base of the mountain
and lit up everything below . . .
the fields, the street, the houses.
Everything.

That night, no one in the town slept.

And ever since then, the night
is full of lights, and people everywhere
can stay up late . . .
looking at the moon
and the stars.

Shadow on the Sun
How a *Pourquoi* Tale Begins

by Franklyn M. Branley

illustrations by Donald Crews

Sometimes the moon hides the sun.

The sky gets dark, almost as dark as night. But it is still daytime.

There is a total solar eclipse. Solar means "of the sun," and eclipse means "to overshadow or leave out."

There is darkness in daytime.

A glow of bright light is around the moon. It is called the solar corona, or the "sun's crown."

During the eclipse, the brightest stars come out. Squirrels and woodchucks get ready to sleep. Birds and chickens go to roost, just as they do at night. If it is springtime, tree frogs start peeping.

Animals are surprised when darkness comes in daytime. Long ago, people were also surprised. Eclipses frightened them.

People thought a dragon in the sky was taking away the sun, eating it bite by bite. The sun might be gone forever.

Everyone made a lot of noise. They shouted and yelled, blew horns and stamped the ground. If they could frighten the dragon, it would spit up the sun.

That's what the dragon did every time. The sun returned. So people continued to believe in the legend of the eclipse dragon.

Thinking About It

1. The man in the story didn't like the night and he wanted to change it. What would you like to change about the world? How would you make your changes?

2. You can travel back in time and visit during a solar eclipse. What do you say to people who think a dragon is eating the sun? Why? How do they answer?

3. You can punch holes in the darkness any way you like. How does your night sky look? How do you show what it looks like to someone else?

How the Ox Star

retold and illustrated by **LILY TOY HONG**

Fell from Heaven

In the beginning, oxen did not live on earth. They could only be found in the heavens, among the stars. They lived with the Emperor of All the Heavens in his Imperial Palace.

Clothed in robes of the finest silk, they reclined on billowy
clouds. They never had to work, and their lives were easy.

Life on earth was hard, especially hard since oxen did not live here. Farmers had no beast of burden to help with the planting of vegetables and rice in the spring or with the gathering of crops at harvest time.

People were always tired and hungry. They labored from sunup to sundown, yet they could never finish all their work. Because there was so little food, they sometimes went three, four, even five days without one single meal.

But the Emperor of All the Heavens had not forgotten the
earth. He knew that the poor peasants worked long and hard,
and he believed that they should be able to eat every third
day. With this in mind, he issued a decree: "The people
of earth shall eat at least once every three days!"

He called upon his most trusted messenger, the Ox Star, to
deliver the message. Dressed in a magnificent silk robe and a
golden crown, the Ox Star set off on the long and lonely
journey down to earth.

When he arrived, all the peasants hurried out to meet him.
"I come with a message from the Emperor of All the Heavens,"
he bellowed. But the Ox Star, while strong, was not very
smart. He twisted the Emperor's words: "The Emperor has
declared that you shall eat three times a day, every day!"
The peasants cheered and cheered.

The Emperor of All the Heavens heard his messenger's mistake and was angry. When the Ox Star arrived back at the Imperial Palace, he found the gates were locked. His princely robe and royal crown vanished. "Since you have betrayed my trust," the Emperor roared, "you shall never again be allowed in the heavens." The sky filled with lightning and thunder, and the Ox Star wept.

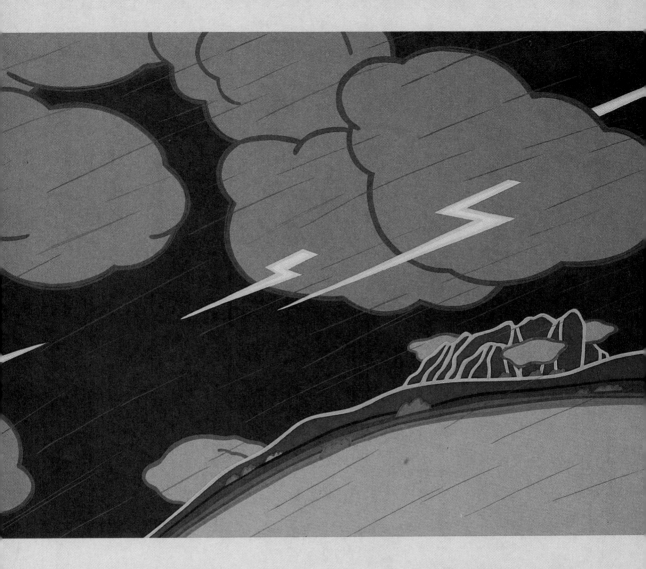

Suddenly, everything turned dark. In a whirlwind, the Ox Star
was hurled through the stormy sky. Down, down, down to
earth he fell.

From that day, the Ox Star became a beast of burden, helping farmers. Around his thick neck he wore a heavy yoke, and through his nose he wore a ring.

The other oxen were sent to earth, too. They labored day after day in the fields, pulling plows through the ground at planting time and helping to gather the crops at harvest time.

Today, because of the Ox Star's ill fortune and his careless mistake, a bit of heaven remains on earth. For those who have an ox, good soil, and enough rain, life is not as hard as it once was. Best of all, they can eat warm rice, tender vegetables, and Chinese sweet cakes three times a day, every day!

Now when you look up at the night sky, so beautiful and bright, think of the Ox Star, who fell from the heavens, and of his blunder, which became a blessing.

How the Ox Star Became a Book

by Lily Toy Hong

When I was in third grade, I never would have thought that many years later third-graders like you would be reading a story I wrote. I have always enjoyed reading folk tales, and I have always been proud to be Chinese. So it may not be too surprising that my very first book is *How the Ox Star Fell from Heaven*, an ancient Chinese folk tale.

The idea for the Ox Star book came to me when I was in college. My class was asked to do drawings about water. After thinking about it, I decided to paint water buffalo. Water buffalo have another name. They are also called oxen. I found many books on water buffalo at the library. I discovered the ancient Chinese myth about how oxen came to Earth. I was delighted with the story, and I thought it

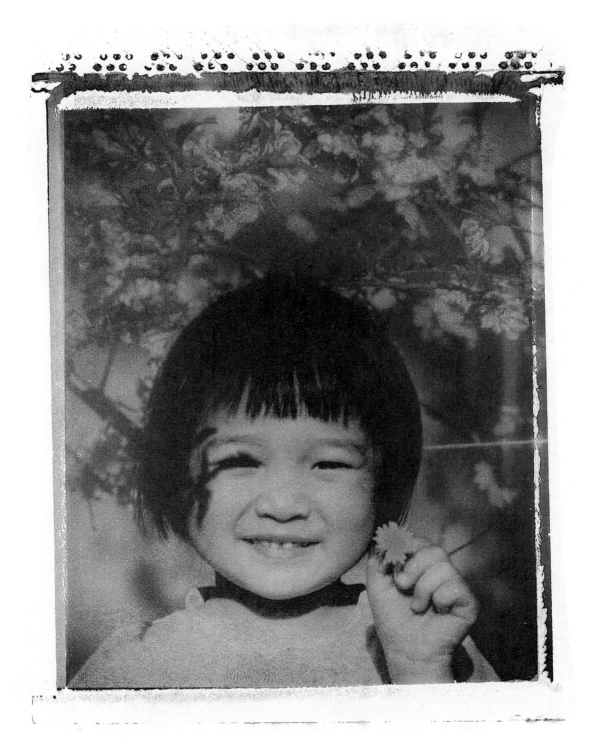

would make a nice picture book. Toward the end of the school year, I turned this idea into a picture book. What do you think? Is it a good picture book?

After graduation, I lived in Taiwan for several years. There I saw farmers working in rice paddies, and I saw oxen pulling plows in the fields. I also saw a lot of Chinese people eating many times a day, which made me very happy.

Then my chance came. My story was to become a published book. More than seven years had passed since my first idea, but the time in between was valuable. My background in art and my experiences in Taiwan came together, and now I am able to share my story with you.

Thinking About It

1. Are you glad the Ox Star fell from heaven? Why?
2. *Pourquoi* tales were told to explain things in the world people could not understand. Do you think these stories make sense? Did they make sense to other people? Tell why you think so.
3. *Pourquoi* tales are stories that tell why something happens. Make a *pourquoi* story to tell why birds have wings, why there is thunder, or why the moon changes shapes.

Keep Wondering Why

Guinea Fowl and Cow discover how nice it is to have friends, especially when there's a hungry lion around, in this Swahili tale called *How the Guinea Fowl Got Her Spots* retold by Barbara Knutson.

The Camel

BY OGDEN NASH

The camel has a single hump;
The dromedary, two;
Or else the other way around.
I'm never sure. Are you?

How to Tell a Camel

BY J. PATRICK LEWIS

The Dromedary has one hump,
The Bactrian has two.

It's easy to forget this rule,
So here is what to do.
Roll the first initial over
On its flat behind:

The Bactrian is different from

The Dromedary kind.

How the Camel Got His Hump

by Rudyard Kipling

Retold as reader's theater by Caroline Feller Bauer

CHARACTERS

NARRATOR 1	DOG
NARRATOR 2	OX
CAMEL	MAN
HORSE	DJINN

NARRATOR 2: We would like to present *How the Camel Got His Hump* by Rudyard Kipling.

NARRATOR 1: *(grandly, in sonorous tones)* In the beginning of years, when the world was so new-and-all and the animals were just beginning to work for man, there was a camel. He lived in the middle of a howling desert because he did not want to work; besides, he was a howler himself.

NARRATOR 2:	So he ate sticks and thorns and tamarisks and milkweed and prickles, most 'scruciating idle. When anybody spoke to him he said,
CAMEL:	Humph!
NARRATOR 2:	Just,
CAMEL:	Humph!
NARRATOR 2:	and no more.
NARRATOR 1:	Presently the horse came to him on Monday morning with a saddle on his back and a bit in his mouth.
HORSE:	Camel, O Camel, come out and trot like the rest of us.
CAMEL:	Humph!
NARRATOR 1:	And the horse went away and told the man.
NARRATOR 2:	Presently the dog came to him with a stick in his mouth.

DOG:	Camel, O Camel, come and fetch and carry like the rest of us.
CAMEL:	Humph!
NARRATOR 2:	And the dog went away and told the man.
NARRATOR 1:	Presently the ox came to him with the yoke on his neck.
OX:	Camel, O Camel, come and plow like the rest of us.
CAMEL:	Humph!
NARRATOR 1:	And the ox went away and told the man.
NARRATOR 2:	At the end of the day the man called the horse and the dog and the ox together.
MAN:	Three, O three, I'm very sorry for you (with the world so new-and-all); but that humph-thing in the desert can't work, or he would have been here by now. I'm going to leave him alone, and you must work doubletime to make up for it.

127

NARRATOR 1: That made the three very angry (with the world so new-and-all), and they held a palaver, and an *indaba*, and a *punchayet*, and a pow-wow on the edge of the desert; and the camel came chewing milkweed *most* 'scruciating idle, and laughed at them.

NARRATOR 2: Then he said,

CAMEL: Humph!

NARRATOR 2: and went away again.

NARRATOR 1: Presently there came along the djinn in charge of all deserts, rolling on a cloud of dust (djinns always travel that way because it is magic), and he stopped to palaver and pow-wow with the three.

HORSE: Djinn of All Deserts: Is it right for anyone to be idle with the world so new-and-all?

DJINN: *(firmly)* Certainly not.

HORSE: Well, there's a thing in the middle of your howling desert (and he's a howler himself) with a long neck and long legs, and he hasn't done a stroke of work since Monday morning. He won't trot.

DJINN: *(whistling)* Whew! That's my camel, for all the gold in Arabia! What does he say about it?

DOG: He says "Humph!" and he won't fetch and carry.

DJINN: Does he say anything else?

OX: Only "Humph!" and he won't plow.

DJINN: Very good. I'll "humph" him if you will kindly wait a minute.

NARRATOR 1: The djinn rolled himself up in his dust cloak, and took a bearing across the desert, and found the camel most 'scruciatingly idle, looking at his own reflection in a pool of water.

DJINN: My long and bubbling friend: What's this I hear of your doing no work with the world so new-and-all?

CAMEL: Humph!

NARRATOR 2: The djinn sat down with his chin in his hand and began to think a great magic, while the camel looked at his own reflection in the pool of water.

DJINN: You've given the three extra work ever since Monday morning, all on account of your 'scruciating idleness.

NARRATOR 1: The djinn went on thinking magics with his chin in his hand.

CAMEL: Humph!

DJINN: I shouldn't say that again if I were you. You might say it once too often. Bubbles, I want you to work.

CAMEL:	Humph!
NARRATOR 2:	No sooner had the camel said,
CAMEL:	Humph!
NARRATOR 2:	than he saw his back, that he was so proud of, puffing up and puffing up into a great big lolloping humph.
DJINN:	Do you see that? That's your very own humph that you've brought upon your very own self by not working. Today is Thursday, and you've done no work since Monday when the work began. Now you are going to work.
CAMEL:	*(whining)* How can I with this humph on my back?

DJINN: That's made a-purpose, all because you missed those three days. You will be able to work now for three days without eating because you can live on your humph. Don't you ever say I never did anything for you. Come out of the desert and go to the three, and behave. Humph yourself!

NARRATOR 1: And the camel humphed himself, humph and all, and went away to join the three. And from that day to this the camel always wears a humph (we call it "hump" now, not to hurt his feelings).

NARRATOR 2: But he has never yet caught up with the three days that he missed at the beginning of the world, and he has never yet learned how to behave.

ALL: Humph!

Pulling It All Together

1. You're going to perform *How the Camel Got His Hump* as a school play. Which character do you want to be? Why?
2. Two friends of yours are having trouble getting along. You'd like to teach them about understanding. Which stories from this book would you want to tell them about?
3. You're having a party and want to invite three of the characters from this book. How could you make up special invitations for these characters? How would you make the invitations different for each one?

Books to Enjoy

Amelia Bedelia
by Peggy Parish

Mr. and Mrs. Rogers have a new maid. It's Amelia Bedelia! When Mrs. Rogers tells Amelia to draw the drapes, dress the chicken, or dust the furniture, she gets some unexpected results!

I Have a Sister, My Sister Is Deaf
by Jeanne Whitehouse Peterson

This sister likes to play the piano, but she can never sing. She can't hear the thunder, but she can sleep through storms. A young girl tells about life with her very special sister.

Hedgehog for Breakfast
by Ann Turner

"I'd like to have Mrs. Hedgehog for breakfast," said Papa. The young foxes can't believe it! What about the prickles? What about the bugs she eats? Find out what's really on the menu in this tale of misunderstandings.

I Hate English
by Ellen Levine

Mei and her family have just moved to New York from China. Everything is in English, and Mei doesn't speak a word of it. How will she ever learn to like this foreign language?

The Drinking Gourd
by F.N. Monjo

A boy learns the secret message of "following the drinking gourd" when he helps slaves escape along the Underground Railroad.

Animals and Where They Live
by John Feltwell

Everything you ever wanted to know about animals and then some! This book is full of colorful pictures which make the world of animals come alive.

The Legend of the Bluebonnet
retold and illustrated by Tomie dePaola

When the Comanche people are suffering from a drought, one little girl decides she will save them.

Literary Terms

First-Person Point of View

In *Mom Can't See Me,* Leslie is telling about her own life with a mother who cannot see. Because Leslie is telling the story as if she were talking to us, we say the author is writing in the **first person.** Notice how she begins: "Nine years ago, when *I* was born . . ." In first-person stories, you will see the word *I* used often.

Multiple Meanings

Some words have more than one meaning, depending on how the word is used. Authors use these **multiple meanings** of words to make a story funny. In "Ramona's Great Day," Miss Binney tells Ramona to "Sit here for the present." What does Ramona think is going to happen? How does Ann Cameron use multiple meanings in "The Pudding Like a Night on the Sea" to make the story funny?

Nonfiction

Nonfiction is written to give you information. "Animal Talk" tells how animals communicate in many ways. You know that dogs bark and growl to send messages such as "I am hungry" and "Get out of my yard." What messages do birds, fireflies, ants, and wolves send? What animal facts did you find out in "On the Trail"?

Play

In some **plays,** the story is told by the narrators and by what the characters say. The narrators give you information about what is happening in the story. The characters each have a part to read. They tell the story through their own words.

Pourquoi Tale

Some stories explain how things in nature came to be. These stories are called *pourquoi tales. Pourquoi* is a French word that means "why." *Pourquoi* tales try to explain why something happens in nature. What do we learn about the stars and the moon when we read *The Night of the Stars*? What do the stories *How the Ox Star Fell from Heaven* and *How the Camel Got His Hump* tell you about nature?

Glossary

Words from your stories

a·maze (ə māz′), to surprise greatly; strike with sudden wonder: *She was amazed at how different the strand of hair looked under a microscope. verb.* **a·maz·es, a·mazed, a·maz·ing.**

blun·der (blun′dər), **1** a stupid mistake: *Misspelling the title of a book is a silly blunder to make in a book report.* **2** to make a stupid mistake: *Someone blundered in sending you to the wrong address.* **3** to move as if blind; stumble: *I blundered through the dark room.* **1** *noun,* **2,3** *verb.*

boom (büm), **1** a deep hollow sound like the roar of cannon or of big waves: *We listened to the boom of the pounding surf.* **2** to make a deep hollow sound: *His voice boomed out above the rest.* **1** *noun,* **2** *verb.*

budge (buj), to move even a little: *The stone was so heavy that we couldn't budge it. verb,* **budg·es, budged, budg·ing.**

care·less (ker′lis *or* kar′lis), **1** not thinking about what you say or do; not careful: *I was careless and broke the cup.* **2** done without enough thought or effort; not exact or thorough: *careless work.* **3** not caring or troubling; indifferent: *Some people are careless about their appearance. adjective.*

chem·i·cal (kem′ə kəl), any substance used in chemistry. Acids, bases, and gases, such as oxygen and hydrogen, are chemicals: *The teacher ordered new chemicals for class experiments. noun.*

com·mu·ni·cate (kə myü′nə kāt), to give or exchange information or news: *Since my brother is away at school, I communicate with him by telephone every weekend. She communicated her wishes to me in a letter. verb,* **com·mu·ni·cates, com·mu·ni·cat·ed, com·mu·ni·cat·ing.**

con·ver·sa·tion (kon′vər sā′shən), a friendly talk; exchange of thoughts by talking informally together: *The two travelers had a nice conversation while waiting for the train. noun.*

cringe (krinj), **1** to crouch in fear; shrink from danger or pain: *The kitten cringed when it saw the dog come into the yard.* **2** to shrink back with embarrassment: *Pat cringed when he forgot the words to his song during the talent show. verb,* **cring·es, cringed, cring·ing.**

conversation
having a **conversation** with a friend

a hat	i it	oi oil	ch child	ə stands for:
ā age	ī ice	ou out	ng long	a in about
ä far	o hot	u cup	sh she	e in taken
e let	ō open	ù put	th thin	i in pencil
ē equal	ô order	ü rule	ᴛʜ then	o in lemon
ėr term			zh measure	u in circus

dou·ble·time (dub′əl tīm′), twice as long as usual: *During wartime, factory shifts often work doubletime to complete orders. adjective.*

du·et (dü et′ *or* dyü et′), **1** a piece of music for two voices or instruments: *Danny and Marcella played a terrific trumpet duet.* **2** two singers or players performing together. *noun.*

em·bar·rass (em bar′əs), make uneasy and ashamed; make self-conscious: *She embarrassed me by asking me if I really liked her. verb.*

fetch (fech), **1** to go and get; bring: *Please fetch me my glasses.* **2** to be sold for: *These eggs will fetch a good price. verb.*

frus·trate (frus′trāt), to defeat; make useless or worthless; block: *Heavy rain frustrated our plans for a picnic. verb,* **frus·trates, frus·trat·ed, frus·trat·ing.**

frus·trat·ed (frus′trā tid), disappointed: *Mel was frustrated when he didn't make the softball team. adjective.* See **frustrate.**

glow (glō), **1** to shine because of heat; be red-hot or white-hot: *Embers still glowed in the fireplace after the fire had died down.* **2** to give off light without heat: *Some clocks glow in the dark.* **3** a bright, warm color: *The glow of the sunset lit the mountaintop.* **1,2** *verb,* **3** *noun.*

har·vest (här′vist), **1** a reaping and gathering in of grain and other food crops: *Father takes on more workers at harvest time.* **2** to gather in and bring home for use: *to harvest wheat.* **3** one season's yield of any natural product; crop: *The clam harvest was small this year.* **1,3** *noun,* **2** *verb.*

howl (houl), **1** to give a long, loud, mournful cry: *Our dog often howls at night. The winter winds howled around our cabin.* **2** a long, loud, mournful cry: *the howl of a wolf.* **3** to yell or shout: *It was so funny that we howled with laughter.* **1,3** *verb,* **2** *noun.*

hump (def. 1)
Some camels have one **hump.**

hump (hump), **1** a rounded lump that sticks out: *Some camels have two humps on their backs.* **2** to raise or bend up into a lump: *The cat humped its back when it saw the dog.* **3** a mound. **1,3** *noun,* **2** *verb.*

humph (humf), an expression that indicates that the speaker is uninterested or insulted: *The snobbish king said "Humph!" when the royal cooks brought him his dinner. interjection.*

in·de·pend·ent (in/di pen/dənt),
  1 thinking or acting for oneself; not
  influenced by others: *Rita has a very
  independent mind and rarely agrees
  with the rest of us.* **2** guiding, ruling, or
  governing oneself; not under another's
  rule: *The United States is an
  independent country. adjective.*

in·for·ma·tion (in/fər mā/shən),
  1 knowledge given or received of some
  fact or event; news: *We have just
  received information that the astronauts
  landed safely.* **2** things known; facts: *A
  dictionary contains much information
  about words. noun.*

insect (def. 1) a grasshopper

in·sect (in/sekt), **1** any of a group of
  small animals without backbones, with
  bodies divided into three parts. Insects
  have three pairs of legs and one or two
  pairs of wings. Flies, mosquitoes,
  butterflies, and bees are insects. **2** any
  similar small animal, especially one
  without wings and with four pairs of
  legs. Spiders and centipedes are often
  called insects. *noun.*

kin·der·gar·ten (kin/dər gärt/n), a
  school for children from about 4 to 6
  years old that educates them by
  games, toys, and pleasant activities:
  *Jeannie will start kindergarten this fall.
  noun.*

lol·lop·ing (lol/əp ing), moving in a
  bounding or leaping manner: *The great
  beast went lolloping over the desert.
  adjective.*

mis·un·der·stand·ing (mis/un/dər
  stan/ding), **1** a wrong understanding;
  failure to understand; mistake as to
  meaning: *A misunderstanding caused
  Reggie to go to the wrong building.*
  2 a disagreement: *After their
  misunderstanding they scarcely spoke
  to each other. noun.*

pair (per *or* par), **1** a set of two; two that
  go together: *I can't find my pair of
  basketball shoes.* **2** a single thing
  consisting of two parts that cannot be
  used separately: *a pair of scissors, a
  pair of trousers. noun, plural* **pairs** or
  pair.

pair (def. 1)
a **pair** of girls

a hat	i it	oi oil	ch child	ə stands for:
ā age	ī ice	ou out	ng long	a in about
ä far	o hot	u cup	sh she	e in taken
e let	ō open	ù put	th thin	i in pencil
ē equal	ô order	ü rule	ŦH then	o in lemon
ėr term			zh measure	u in circus

paw (pô), **1** the foot of a four-footed animal having claws. Cats and dogs have paws. **2** to strike or scrape with the paws or feet: *The cat pawed the mouse it had caught.* **3** to handle awkwardly or roughly: *Stop pawing the tomatoes, or you'll bruise them.* **1** *noun,* **2,3** *verb.*

peak (pēk), **1** the pointed top of a mountain or hill: *We could see for miles from the mountain peak.* **2** mountain that stands alone: *Pikes Peak.* **3** any pointed end or top: *the peak of a roof.* **4** the highest point: *reach the peak of one's profession.* **5** the front part or the brim of a cap that stands out. *noun.*

peak (def. 1)
jagged mountain **peaks**

pes·ter (pes/tər), to annoy; trouble: *Flies pester us. Don't pester me with foolish questions.* *verb.*

plant (plant), **1** any living thing that can make its own food from sunlight, air, and water. Plants cannot move about by themselves. Trees, bushes, vines, grass, vegetables, and seaweed are all plants. **2** to put in the ground to grow: *She planted sunflower seeds in the backyard.* **1** *noun,* **2** *verb.*

plow (plou), **1** a big, heavy farm instrument for cutting the soil and turning it over: *We repaired the broken plows in time for the spring planting.* **2** to turn up the soil with a plow: *to plow a field.* **3** to move through anything as a plow does; advance slowly and with effort: *The ship plowed through the waves.* **1** *noun,* **2,3** *verb.* Also spelled **plough.**

plow (def. 1)
a tractor pulling a **plow**

poke (pōk), **1** to push against with something pointed; jab: *He poked me in the ribs with his elbow.* **2** to thrust; push: *The dog poked its head out of the car window.* **3** to go in a lazy way; loiter: *She felt tired and just poked around the house all day.* *verb,* **pokes, poked, pok·ing.**

pud·ding (pùd/ing), a soft, cooked food, usually sweet, such as rice pudding: *Maggie's favorite dessert is lemon pudding. noun.*

punch (punch), **1** to hit with the fists: *Alex punched his pillow to fluff it up.* **2** a quick thrust or blow: *The fighter took a punch to the jaw.* **3** to pierce a hole in: *The conductor punched the ticket.* **1,3** *verb,* **2** *noun, plural* **punch·es, punched.**

re·flec·tion (ri flek′shən), **1** the throwing back of light, heat, sound, or the like: *The reflection of sunlight by sand and water can cause a sunburn.* **2** a likeness; image: *I looked at my reflection in the mirror. noun.*

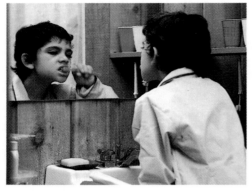

reflection (def. 2)

rule (rül), **1** a statement of what to do and what not to do; principle governing conduct or action: *Obey the rules of the game.* **2** to decide: *My parents ruled in my favor in the dispute between my sister and me. The judge ruled against them.* **3** to control; govern: *The majority rules in a democracy.* 1 *noun,* 2,3 *verb,* **rules, ruled, rul·ing.**
as a rule, usually: *As a rule, hail falls in summer rather than in winter.*
rule out, to decide against: *He did not rule out a possible camping trip this summer.*

sig·nal (sig′nəl), **1** a sign giving notice of something: *A red light is a signal of danger.* **2** to make a signal or signals to: *She signaled the car to stop by raising her hand.* 1 *noun,* 2 *verb.*
spe·cial (spesh′əl), **1** of a particular kind; distinct from others; not general: *A safe has a special lock. Have you any special color in mind for your new coat?* **2** more than ordinary; unusual; exceptional: *Lions and tigers hold special interest for many students.* **3** having a particular purpose, function, or use: *Send the letter by a special messenger. adjective.*
spill (spil), **1** to let liquid or any loose matter run or fall: *Rusty spilled the gravy on the floor.* **2** to fall or flow out: *Water spilled from the pail.* **3** a fall: *He took a bad spill trying to ride that horse.* 1,2 *verb,* **spills, spilled** or **spilt, spill·ing;** 3 *noun.*

taste (tāst), **1** flavor; what is special about something to the sense organs of the mouth. Sweet, sour, salt, and bitter are the four most important tastes. *I think this milk is sour; it has a funny taste.* **2** to try the flavor of something by taking a little into the mouth: *The cook tastes everything to see if it is right.* **3** to have a particular flavor: *The soup tastes of onion.* **4** a little bit; sample: *Give me just a taste of the pudding. The snowstorm will give you a taste of northern winter.* 1,4 *noun,* 2,3 *verb,* **tastes, tast·ed, tast·ing.**

a hat	i it	oi oil	ch child	ə stands for:
ā age	ī ice	ou out	ng long	a in about
ä far	o hot	u cup	sh she	e in taken
e let	ō open	ù put	th thin	i in pencil
ē equal	ô order	ü rule	ŦH then	o in lemon
ėr term			zh measure	u in circus

tired (tīrd), weary; wearied; exhausted: *I'm tired, but I must get back to work.* *adjective.*

touch (tuch), **1** to put the hand or some other part of the body on or against and feel: *I touched the soft, furry kitten.* **2** the sense by which a person perceives things by feeling, handling, or coming against them: *Some animals have a keen sense of touch.* **3** communication; connection: *She kept in touch with her family while she was overseas.* **1** *verb,* **2,3** *noun, plural* **touch·es.**

track (trak), **1** a pair of parallel metal rails for cars to run on: *railroad tracks.* **2** a mark left: *The dirt road showed many automobile tracks.* **3** a footprint: *We saw bear tracks near the camp.* **4** to follow by means of footprints, smell, or any mark left by anything that has passed by: *We tracked the deer and photographed it.* **5** a course for running or racing. **1-3,5** *noun,* **4** *verb.*

trans·late (tran slāt′), to change from one language into another: *The teacher asked the students to translate the chapter from French into English. verb,* **trans·lates, trans·lat·ed, trans·lat·ing.**

trans·la·tor (tran slā′tər), a person who translates: *Najeeb works as a translator at the United Nations. noun.* See **translate.**

trip (trip), **1** a journey; voyage: *Our neighbors took a trip to Europe.* **2** to stumble: *He tripped on the stairs.* **3** to make a mistake; do something wrong: *He tripped on that difficult question.* **1** *noun,* **2,3** *verb,* **trips, tripped, trip·ping.**

un·fair (un fer′ *or* un far′), unjust: *an unfair decision. It was unfair of you to trick him. adjective.*

track (def. 5)

Acknowledgments

Text

Pages 6–14: From *The Stories Julian Tells* by Ann Cameron, illustrations by Ann Strugnell. Text copyright © 1981 by Ann Cameron. Illustrations copyright © 1981 by Ann Strugnell. Reprinted by permission of Pantheon Books, a division of Random House, Inc.
Page 16–32: "Ramona's Great Day" from *Ramona the Pest* by Beverly Cleary, illustrated by Louis Darling. Copyright © 1968 by Beverly Cleary. Reprinted by permission of William Morrow & Company, Inc.
Pages 34–35: "Sing Me a Song of Teapots and Trumpets" from *Hurry, Hurry, Mary Dear! and Other Nonsense Poems* by N. M. Bodecker. Copyright © 1976 by N. M. Bodecker. Reprinted by permission of Margaret K. McElderry Books, an imprint of Macmillan Publishing Company.
Pages 36–51: *Mom Can't See Me* by Sally Hobart Alexander. Text copyright © 1990 by Sally Hobart Alexander. Reprinted by permission of Macmillan Publishing Company.
Pages 52–54: "A Message from Mom" by Sally Hobart Alexander. Copyright © 1991 by Sally Hobart Alexander.
Pages 56–68: From *Singing Birds and Flashing Fireflies* by Dorothy Hinshaw Patent. Text copyright © 1989 by Dorothy Hinshaw Patent. All rights reserved. Reprinted by permission of Franklin Watts, New York.
Pages 70–82: From *Animal Tracks and Traces*. Copyright © 1991 by Kathleen V. Kudlinski. Reprinted with permission of the publisher, Franklin Watts, Inc.
Pages 84–97: *The Night of the Stars* by Douglas Gutiérrez and María Fernanda Oliver. Translated by Carmen Diana Dearden. Copyright © 1987 Ediciones Ekaré-Banco del Libro. Reprinted by permission of Kane/Miller Book Publishers.
Pages 98–100: From *Eclipse: Darkness in Daytime* by Franklyn Branley, illustrated by Donald Crews. Text copyright © 1988, 1973 by Franklyn M. Branley. Illustration copyright © 1988, 1973 by Donald Crews. Reprinted by permission of HarperCollins*Publishers*.
Pages 102–117: *How the Ox Star Fell from Heaven* by Lily Toy Hong. Copyright © 1991 by Lily Toy Hong.

Used by permission of Albert Whitman & Company.
Pages 118–120: "How the Ox Star Became a Book" by Lily Toy Hong. Copyright © 1991 by Lily Toy Hong.
Page 122: "The Camel" from *Verses from 1929 On* by Ogden Nash. Copyright © 1933 by Ogden Nash. First appeared in *The Saturday Evening Post*. Reprinted by permission of Little, Brown and Company.
Page 123: "How to Tell a Camel" from *A Hippopotamusn't and Other Animal Verses* by J. Patrick Lewis. Copyright © 1985 by J. Patrick Lewis. Used by permission of Dial Books for Young Readers, a division of Penguin Books USA Inc.

Artists

Illustrations owned and copyrighted by the illustrator.
Tom Curry, cover, 1–5, 133, 134–135, 144
Ann Strugnell, 6, 8, 9, 12, 15
Louis Darling, 16, 19, 22, 25, 33
N. M. Bodecker, 34–35
John Burgoyne, 56–69, 137
Geoffrey Moss, 70–83
María Fernanda Oliver, 84–97
Donald Crews, 98–101
Lily Toy Hong, 102–117, 121
Jennie Oppenheimer, 122–132, 136–137,
John Morrison (photo treatments), 119, 120

Photographs

Unless otherwise acknowledged, all photographs are the property of Scott Foresman.
Pages 36–51, 55: George Ancona
Page 53: Courtesy of Sally Hobart Alexander
Pages 119, 120: Courtesy of Lily Toy Hong
Page 140L: Lenore Weber
Page 141L: Dale Jorgenson/Tom Stack and Associates
Page 141R: Food and Drug Department/U.S. Dept. of Agriculture
Page 143: Information Canada Phototheque

Glossary

The contents of the Glossary have been adapted from *Beginning Dictionary*, Copyright © 1988, Scott, Foresman and Company.